Tea Time
Tidbits
and Treats

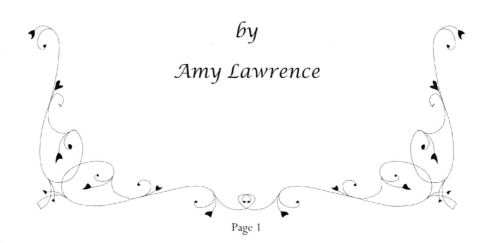

by

Amy Lawrence

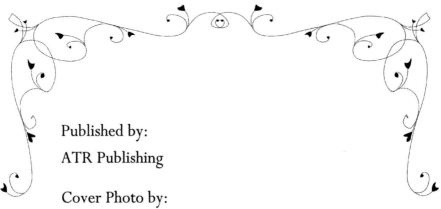

Published by:
ATR Publishing

Cover Photo by:
Rob Macklin

Back Cover Photo by:
Sirlin Photographers
(916)444-8464
http://www.sirlin.com/

ISBN: 978-0-9796170-3-4

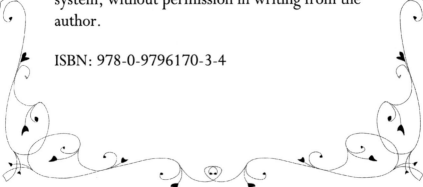

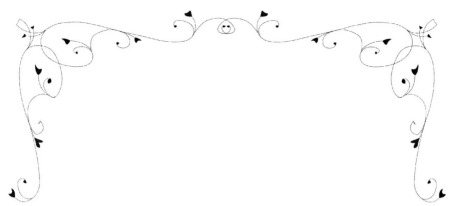

An Afternoon to Remember is dedicated to educating others in the art of taking tea. Our mission is to provide a unique upscale experience where customers are pampered and can relax, socialize and celebrate special occasions while enjoying excellent teas and delectable treats. Tea rooms entice you to sit leisurely, and this is the main goal and purpose of our tea room making your experience here truly...

"An Afternoon to Remember."

Forward

Every year I publish a cookbook with new recipes. I could never have done this without the help of my staff. Everyone is so committed to our tea room. They bring in ideas, add constructive criticism and treat my business as if it is their own. I am so proud of them! From creating the recipes, to perfecting them, to editing, and designing the cookbook, I want to thank them all for their hard work! I would also like to thank my wonderful customers. They often give us inspiration for new recipes.

This cookbook is the combination of everyone's efforts – Carla Sherman, Alejandra Sanchez, Connie Johnson, Dena Macklin, Patti Schmicking, Fran Swart and a dear customer, Arnelle Sanford. However, without Carla, Alejandra, Connie and Dena, this cookbook would have never been written. They are the ones who actually experiment and create these delicious recipes day after day. Thank you all so much!

Last but not least, is my wonderful husband, Pat. He puts up with all of my late nights, long weekends and whining. He is the reason this

Forward Continued

book ever gets put together. Without my computer genius, I would be lost. Thank you sweetie! Pat has worked extremely hard on this one as it is published by our new company, ATR Publishing. After 3 years of self-publishing our cookbooks with a local printer, I was encouraged by eWomen Publishing Network to branch out and actually have it really "published" So this is it! Our first cookbook published under our own company. We're so proud!

I hope you enjoy the recipes in this cookbook and that they inspire you to create your own recipes. Happy cooking!

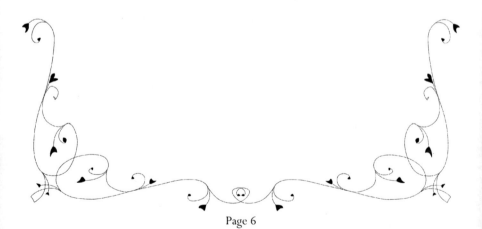

Table of Contents

Tea and Such

Tea Sandwiches

Table of Contents Continued

Tea Sandwiches

Soups and Salads

Desserts

Table of Contents Continued

Desserts

Scones and Condiments

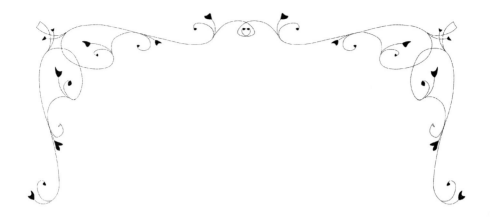

Tea and Such

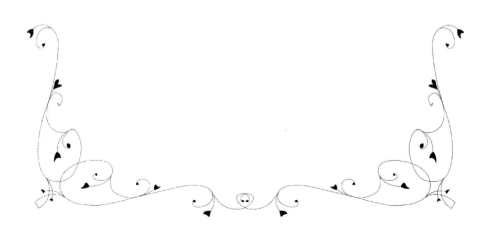

The Perfect Pot of Black Tea

Fill kettle with freshly drawn cold water.

Temper teapot by filling with hot water.

Bring kettle to boil.

Pour out water in teapot.

Place tea sock in teapot.

Add one scant teaspoon of tea per cup.

Pour boiling water over leaves.

Replace teapot lid.

Steep for 3-5 minutes for black tea.

Decant or remove tea sock with leaves.

Stir and serve.

Cover with a tea cozy or use a warmer to keep tea piping hot.

Enjoy!

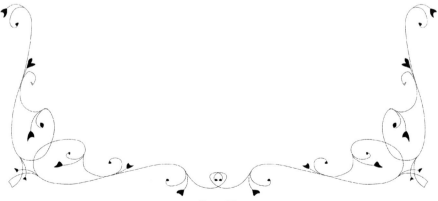

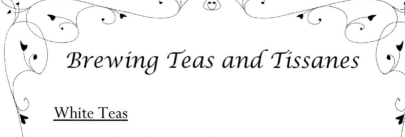

Brewing Teas and Tissanes

White Teas

Water – hot, about 180°
Steeping time – White teas are very mild. To get the full flavor, steep for 10-12 minutes.

Green Teas

Water – hot, about 180°
Steeping time – Most green teas can be steeped more than once. If multiple infusions are desired then start with a steeping time of 2 minutes and then increase it by 1 minute for every additional infusion.

Oolongs

Water – a little less than boiling – around 195°
Steeping time – same as green teas

Black Tea

Water – almost boiling
Steeping time – normally 3-4 minutes. Some Darjeelings are best at 3 minutes.

Brewing Teas and Tissanes Continued

Flavored Black Teas

Water – almost boiling
Steeping time – 3-4 minutes

Tisanes or Herbal Blends

Water – boiling

Steeping time – 7 minutes

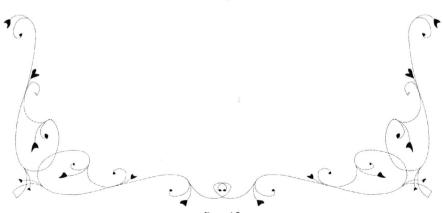

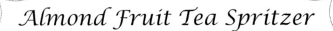

Almond Fruit Tea Spritzer

This is a twist on our almond fruit tea. It makes a nice punch for bridal and baby showers. We served it on Mother's Day and everyone loved it and wanted the recipe. It does have a lot of sugar, feel free to cut down on the sugar amount if you wish.

- 3 T. loose Assam tea
- 4 cups of boiling water, plus enough cold water to fill a one gallon container
- 1 c. sugar (start with ½ c. cup and add the rest to taste, this is a very sweet tea)
- 1 6 oz. can frozen lemonade
- 2 t. almond extract
- 2 qt. chilled ginger ale

Place loose tea in a tea sock or tea infuser. Pour boiling water over the tea leaves. Steep for 4 minutes. Remove leaves from tea. In a one gallon container mix sugar, lemonade and almond extract. Add hot tea. Stir until sugar is dissolved. Fill the container with cold water and/or ice until it reaches half full (2 qts.) Chill. Immediately before serving, add the ginger ale. Serve immediately.

Notes

Almond Fruit Tea Spritzer
Continued

This tea is also good by itself without the ginger ale.

Makes about 1 gallon.

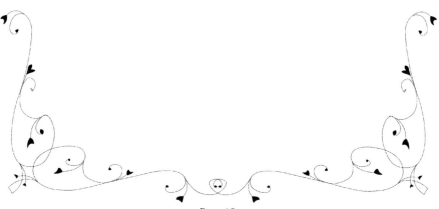

Notes

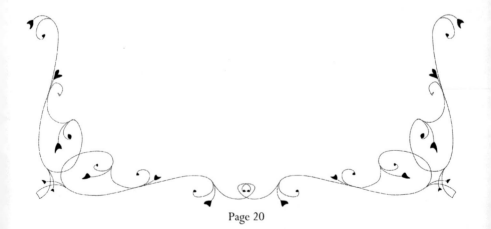

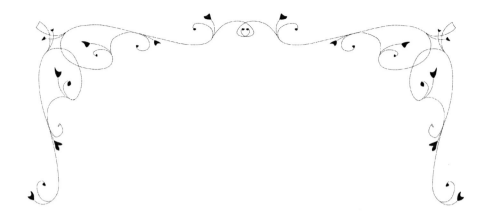

Tea Sandwiches

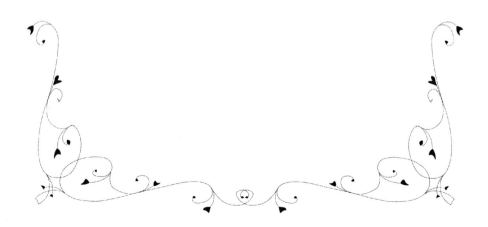

Tips on Making Tea Sandwiches

Make your sandwich fillings ahead of time - most can be made up to 3 days in advance.

If you are making chicken, always use fresh chicken, not canned.

If you are making a tea sandwich with cream cheese filling, always soften the cream cheese before making the filling. Add freshly chopped herbs whenever possible. If you use a little sour cream in the cream cheese mixture, it will make your filling easier to spread.

Always butter the bread before spreading on the filling, otherwise the filling will "leak" through.

Make your sandwiches the day before. Wrap well. Cut them the day of your event. The filling will be cold and solidified so they will slice nicely. If you do them the same day, it's hard to get a "clean" edge.

Use fresh herbs, or chopped veggies for garnish. If you're making an olive sandwich, slice an olive and garnish on top. Always garnish the day of the event for the best look.

Tips on Making Tea Sandwiches Continued

Extra Tips:
* Don't press down when you cut.
* Try to handle them as little as possible.

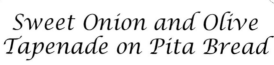

Sweet Onion and Olive Tapenade on Pita Bread

- 8 oz. cream cheese, softened
- ½ c. sweet onions, finely chopped
- 1¾ c. kalamata olives, pitted and chopped
- 2 T. capers
- 3 T. fresh lemon juice
- 2 T. olive oil
- 1 T. fresh parsley, chopped
- 1 T. fresh oregano, chopped
- ¼ t. lemon zest
- 1 clove garlic, crushed and minced
- Freshly ground pepper to taste
- 2 T. red and orange bell peppers, chopped
- 4 pitas, toasted and cut into 8 pie wedges

In food processor beat cream cheese until smooth. Add onions, olives, capers, lemon juice, olive oil, parsley, oregano, zest, garlic, pepper and peppers. Mix well. Spread on toasted pita slices.

Makes about 32 pita wedges.

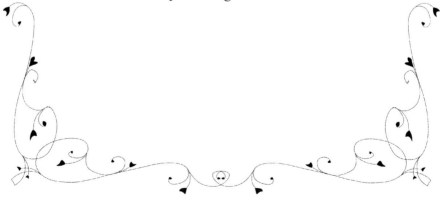

Notes

Mediterranean Cucumber Tea Sandwiches

- 1 8 oz. cream cheese
- ½ c. sour cream
- ½ c. kalamata olives
- ½ c. roasted red pepper, drained
- ¼ c. freshly chopped basil, chopped
- ¾ c. feta cheese
- Salt and pepper to taste
- Garlic powder to taste
- Cucumber slices – rinsed and patted dry
- Butter
- 8 slices of bread of choice, dill rye and dark rye work well

Beat cream cheese until smooth. Add olives, red pepper, basil, and feta. Combine well. Fold in sour cream. Add salt, pepper and garlic powder to taste. Butter 1 slice of bread. Spread cream cheese mixture on slice. Cut each sandwich into 4 squares. Top each with a slice of cucumber. Sprinkle lightly with more pepper.

Makes about 32 tea sandwiches.

Notes

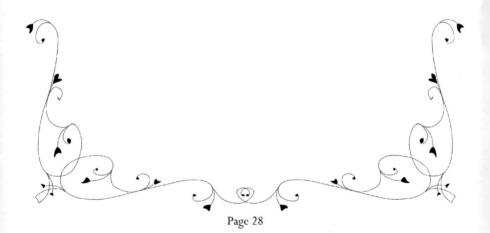

Cucumber Garden Vegetable Tea Sandwiches

- 1 8 oz. pkg cream cheese softened
- ½ c. sour cream
- ½ c. carrot, shredded
- ½ c. zucchini, shredded
- 1 T. fresh parsley, chopped
- ½ t. seasoning salt
- ½ t. garlic powder
- Dash of pepper
- ½ c. water chestnuts, drained and chopped
- 1 cucumber, thinly sliced
- Butter
- 8 slices dark rye, or dill rye bread

Combine cream cheese, carrot, zucchini, parsley, salt, garlic powder, pepper and water chestnuts. Add enough sour cream to desired spreading consistency. Butter a slice of bread. Spread cream cheese mixture on bread slices. Trim off crusts and cut into desired shapes – long rectangles, squares, etc. Top with a cucumber slice. Enjoy!

Makes about 32 tea sandwiches.

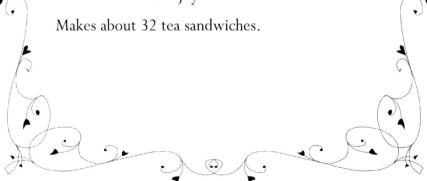

Notes

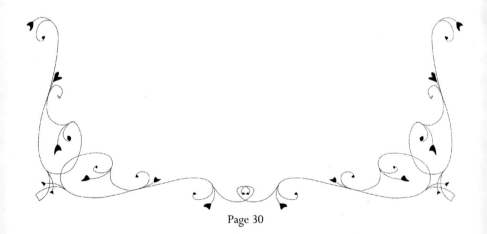

Artichoke Cucumber Tea Sandwiches

- 1 8 oz. pkg. cream cheese
- ½ c. sour cream
- ¼ c. feta
- 1 c. marinated artichoke hearts-drained and chopped
- ⅓ c. red pepper, finely chopped
- 3 green onions, finely chopped
- 1 large clove garlic, crushed
- 1 t. dried tarragon leaves, crushed
- ½ t. dried basil leaves, crushed
- 1 cucumber, sliced
- Butter
- 8 slices rye or pumpernickel bread

Beat cream cheese until smooth. Add feta, artichoke hearts, pepper, green onions, garlic, tarragon and basil. Combine well. Fold in sour cream. Butter 1 slice of bread. Spread cream cheese mixture on slice. Cut each sandwich into 4 squares. Top each with a slice of cucumber. Sprinkle lightly with black pepper if desired.

Makes about 32 tea sandwiches.

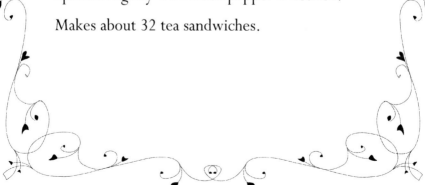

Notes

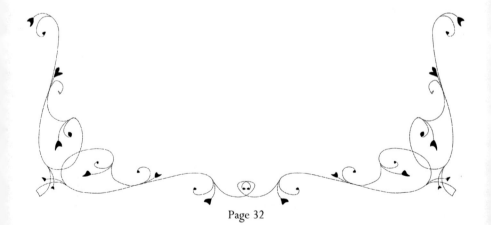

Artichoke with Tomato Tea Sandwiches

- 1 8 oz. pkg cream cheese
- ¼ c. sour cream
- 1 c. marinated artichokes, well-drained
- ½ c. mozzarella
- ½ c. parmesan
- 2-3 cloves of garlic, minced
- 1 tomato, sliced into small pieces for garnish
- 8 slices dill rye bread
- Black pepper

Beat cream cheese until smooth. Add artichokes, cheeses and garlic. Combine well. Fold in sour cream. Butter 1 slice of bread. Spread cream cheese mixture on slice. Cut each sandwich into 4 squares. Top each with a slice of tomato. Sprinkle lightly with black pepper if desired.

Makes about 32 tea sandwiches.

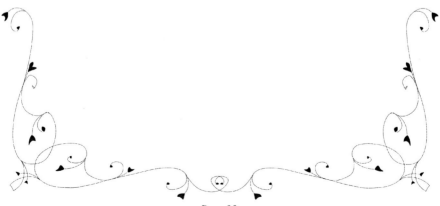

Notes

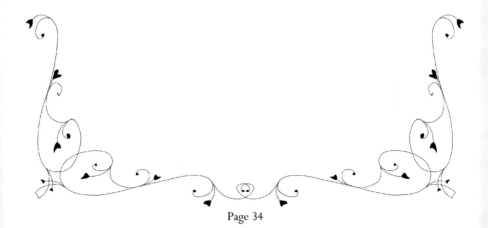

Artichoke Chicken Tea Sandwiches

- 2 c. cooked chicken – pulse lightly in food processor or chop finely
- 3 T. green onions, sliced thinly
- ¾ c. feta cheese
- ½ c. marinated artichoke hearts
- 1 chopped red pepper
- 1 lg. clove garlic, minced
- 1 t. dried and crushed tarragon
- ½ t. dried and crushed basil
- Salt to taste
- Mayonnaise
- Butter
- 8 slices of buttermilk bread
- Parsley for decoration

Mix together first 9 ingredients. Add just enough mayonnaise to bind the mixture together. Spread butter on bread. Add filling and top with second slice. Cut into 4 triangles. Sprinkle parsley on sides of sandwiches for decoration if desired.

Makes about 16 tea sandwiches depending on the thickness of filling and size of the sandwiches.

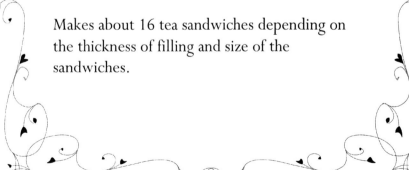

Notes

Roast Beef Tea Sandwiches

- 1 8oz. package cream cheese, softened
- ¼ cup onion, finely chopped
- ¼ cup water chestnuts, finely chopped
- 1 T. mustard
- 2 t. prepared horseradish
- ⅛ t. salt
- Dash pepper
- ¾ c. shaved roast beef, chopped
- 8 slices of Pumpernickel bread or Rye bread
- Butter

Combine cheese, onion, water chestnuts, mustard, horseradish, salt and pepper. Stir in roast beef. Spread 4 slices of bread with butter. Spread half with roast beef mixture and top with remaining halves. Trim off crusts and cut into 4 squares.

Makes about 16 tea sandwiches.

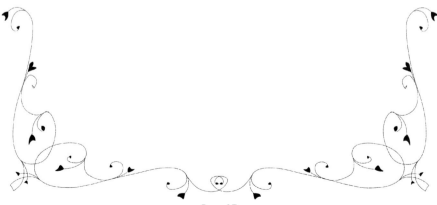

Notes

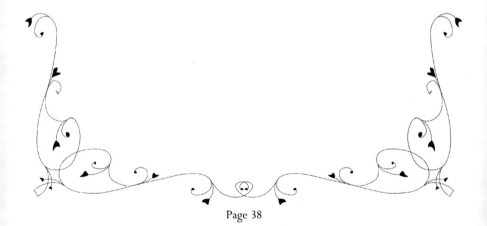

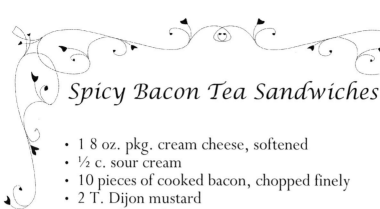

Spicy Bacon Tea Sandwiches

- 1 8 oz. pkg. cream cheese, softened
- ½ c. sour cream
- 10 pieces of cooked bacon, chopped finely
- 2 T. Dijon mustard
- 1 envelope of onion soup mix
- 4-5 T. horseradish or to taste
- ¼ c. sharp cheddar cheese, shredded (optional)
- Butter
- 8 slices dark rye or light rye bread slices

Beat cream cheese until smooth. Add bacon, mustard, soup mix, horseradish and cheese. Combine well. Fold in sour cream. Butter 1 slice of bread. Spread cream cheese mixture on slice. Cut each sandwich into 4 squares or desired shapes. Top each with a slice of tomato. Sprinkle lightly with black pepper if desired.

Makes about 32 tea sandwiches.

Notes

Italian Salami and Cheese Tea Sandwiches

This is a very unique looking sandwich if you can find the marble rye bread.

- 1 8 oz. pkg cream cheese, softened
- ¼ c. sour cream
- ¾ c. salami, finely chopped
- 3 green onions, finely chopped
- ½ c. sharp cheddar cheese, shredded
- 8 marble rye bread slices
- Butter

Combine cream cheese, salami, green onions, and cheese. Fold in sour cream. Spread 4 slices of bread with butter. Spread salami mixture on slices and top with remaining halves. Trim off crusts and cut each sandwich into 3 strips.

Makes about 12 tea sandwiches.

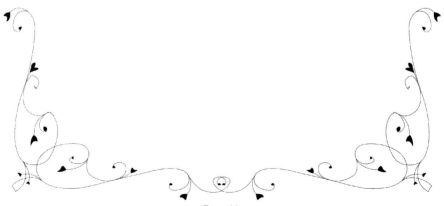

Notes

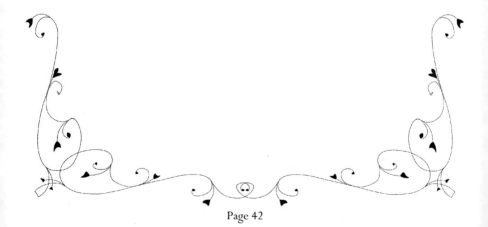

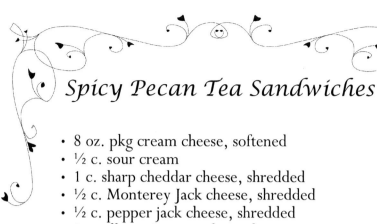

Spicy Pecan Tea Sandwiches

- 8 oz. pkg cream cheese, softened
- ½ c. sour cream
- 1 c. sharp cheddar cheese, shredded
- ½ c. Monterey Jack cheese, shredded
- ½ c. pepper jack cheese, shredded
- 1 small jar pimento, drained
- 1 t. tabasco
- ¼ c. finely chopped spicy pecans – recipe to follow
- Spicy pecans for garnish
- Black pepper to taste
- 8 whole grain bread slices
- Butter

Beat cream cheese until smooth. Add cheeses, pimento, Tabasco and pecans. Combine well. Fold in sour cream. Add black pepper to taste. Butter 1 slice of bread. Spread cream cheese mixture on slice. Cut each sandwich into 4 squares. Top each with a spicy pecan half.

Makes about 32 tea sandwiches.

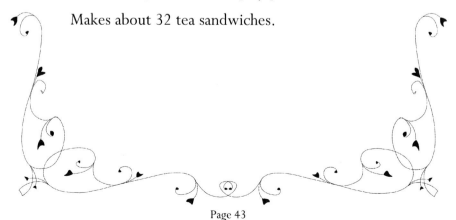

Notes

Spicy Pecans

- 1 T. butter, melted
- 2-3 t. Tabasco
- ½ t. chili powder
- 1 t. garlic powder
- ¼ t. cayenne pepper
- 1 c. pecan halves

Place all ingredients in a bowl. Toss well. Spread on a cookie sheet and bake at 350° for 10 minutes. Check and stir pecans halfway through baking.

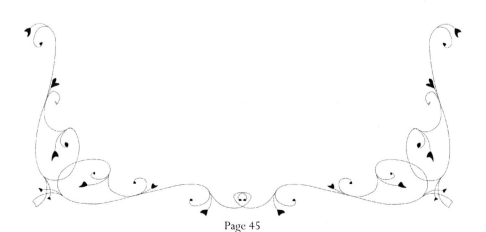

Notes

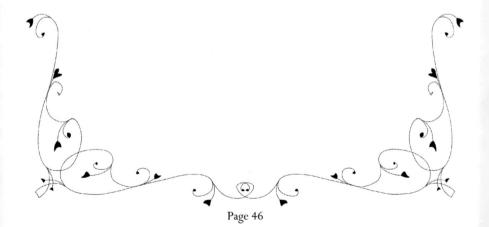

Hearty Herb Cheese Tea Sandwiches

- 8 oz. cream cheese, softened
- ½ c. sour cream
- 1 c. shredded sharp cheddar cheese
- ¼ c. parsley, fresh
- ½ t. dried basil or 2 t. fresh
- ½ t. dried tarragon or 2 t. fresh
- 1 pkg. onion soup mix
- 8 dill bread slices
- Dill sprigs, tomato or cucumber slices, for garnish

In food processor beat cream cheese until smooth. Fold in sour cream. Add cheddar cheese, parsley, basil, tarragon, soup mix and mix well. Spread butter on slice of bread. Spread the herb mixture on top. Cut into 4 squares. Garnish with dill sprig, tomato or cucumber if desired.

Makes about 32 tea sandwiches.

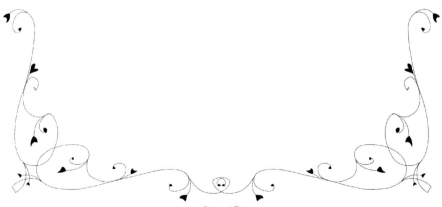

Notes

Blue Cheese Walnut Tea Sandwiches

- 8 oz. cream cheese, softened
- ½ c. sour cream
- ½ c. chopped walnuts, toasted
- ½ c. crumbled blue cheese
- Dash of pepper to taste
- Butter
- 8 dark rye bread slices
- Walnut halves, for garnish

In food processor beat cream cheese until smooth. Fold in sour cream. Add walnuts, blue cheese and pepper, mix well. Spread butter on slice of bread. Spread mixture on top. Cut into 4 squares. Garnish with walnut half if desired.

Makes about 32 tea sandwiches.

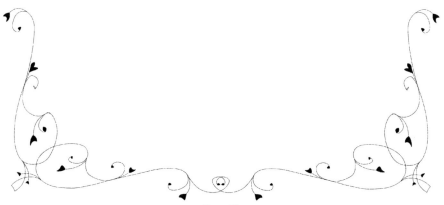

Notes

Tropical Fruit Tea Sandwiches

- 1 8 oz. cream cheese
- ½ c. sour cream
- 3 T. lime juice
- 1 t. honey
- ½ t. cumin
- ¼ t. Tabasco
- ½ c. shredded coconut
- Pineapple slices for garnish
- Cinnamon and sugar for garnish
- Cinnamon bread, cut into rounds

Beat cream cheese until smooth. Add lime juice, honey, cumin, Tabasco, and coconut. Combine well. Fold in sour cream. Spread cream cheese mixture on cinnamon bread round. Top each with a slice of pineapple. Sprinkle with cinnamon and sugar.

Makes about 32 tea sandwiches.

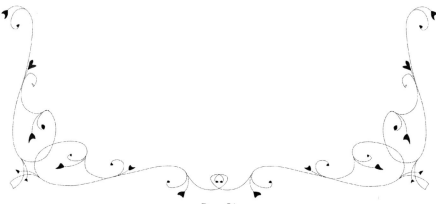

Notes

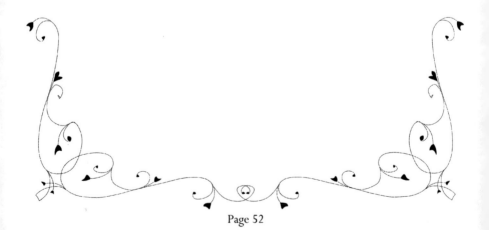

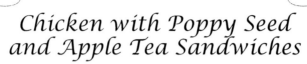

Chicken with Poppy Seed and Apple Tea Sandwiches

- 2 c. cooked chicken
- 2 green onions, sliced thinly
- ½ c. chopped green apple
- 3 T. celery, finely chopped
- 1 t. lemon juice
- 1 t. honey
- 1 t. poppy seeds
- ½ c. mild cheddar cheese (optional)
- Mayo
- 8 buttermilk bread slices
- Butter
- Dried parsley and poppy seeds for garnish

Mix together first 8 ingredients. Add just enough mayonnaise to bind the mixture together. Spread butter on bread. Add filling and top with second slice. Cut into 4 triangles. Sprinkle parsley mixed with poppy seeds on sides of sandwiches for decoration if desired.

Makes about 16 tea sandwiches depending on thickness of filling and size of sandwiches.

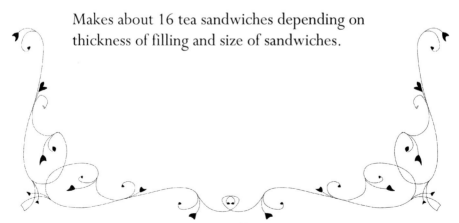

Notes

Ham and Cheese Pinwheels

- 8 oz. cream cheese, softened
- ½ c. sour cream
- 1 c. Black forest ham
- ½ c. shredded cheddar cheese
- 2 c. garlic, minced
- 1 pkg. medium sized tortillas

In food processor, beat cream cheese until smooth. Add sour cream, ham, cheese, and garlic. Blend well. Spread mixture evenly on tortilla. With end of tortilla, roll up tight and evenly. Chill overnight. Cut off end of tortilla and slice into ½ inch slices.

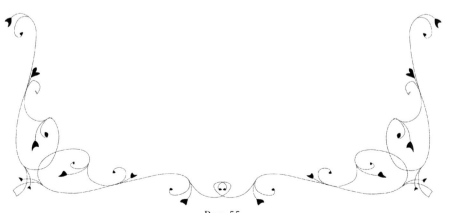

Notes

Blue Cheese Walnut Chicken and Grape Tea Sandwiches

- 2 c. cooked chicken, pulsed lightly in food processor or finely chopped
- 3 T. green onions, finely chopped
- ¼ c. blue cheese
- ½ c. red seedless grapes
- ½ c. walnuts, chopped
- Salt to taste
- Mayonnaise
- 8 slices buttermilk bread
- Dried parsley for decoration

Mix together first 6 ingredients. Add just enough mayonnaise to bind the mixture together. Spread butter on bread. Add filling and top with second slice. Cut into desired shapes. Sprinkle parsley on sides of sandwiches for decoration if desired.

Makes about 16 tea sandwiches depending on the thickness of filling and size of the sandwiches.

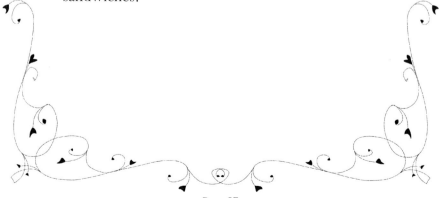

Notes

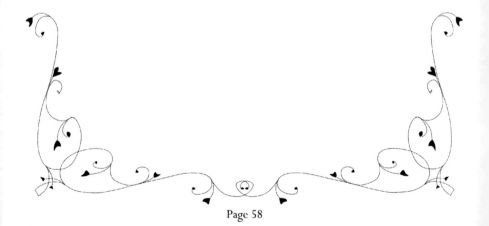

Sesame Cilantro Tea Sandwiches

- 1 8 oz. pkg cream cheese, softened
- ½ c. sour cream
- ¼ c. sesame seeds, toasted
- 4 T. soy sauce
- ¼ c. fresh cilantro, must be fresh!
- 8 slices of dark rye bread
- Butter

In food processor, beat cream cheese until smooth. Add sour cream, sesame seeds, soy sauce and cilantro. Blend well. Spread butter on slices of bread. Spread mixture evenly on bread slices. Cut into 4 squares. Garnish with a cilantro leaf.

Makes about 32 tea sandwiches.

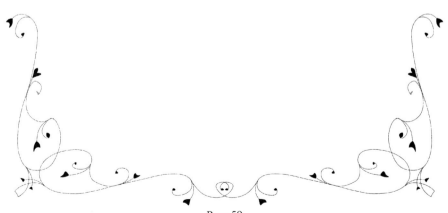

Notes

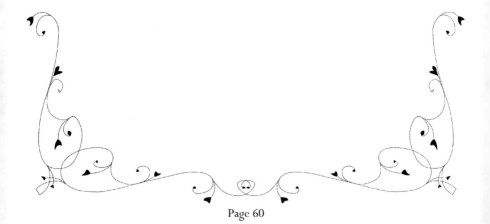

Pine Nut Pimento and Cheese

- 1 8oz. pkg. cream cheese
- ½ c. sour cream
- ½ c. toasted pine nuts
- 3 T. green pepper, finely chopped
- ¾ c. parmesan cheese, shredded
- 1 T. red onion
- 1 small jar of pimento, well-drained
- Slices of red pepper for garnish
- 8 slices of bread of choice, dill rye and dark rye work well

Combine cream cheese, pine nuts, green pepper, parmesan cheese, red onion and pimento. Add enough sour cream to desired spreading consistency. Butter a slice of bread. Spread cream cheese mixture on bread slices. Wrap and chill for a few hours or overnight. Trim off crusts and cut into desired shapes – long rectangles, squares, etc. Top with a red pepper slice. Enjoy!

Makes about 32 tea sandwiches.

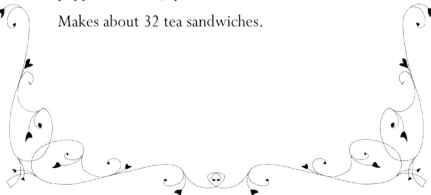

Notes

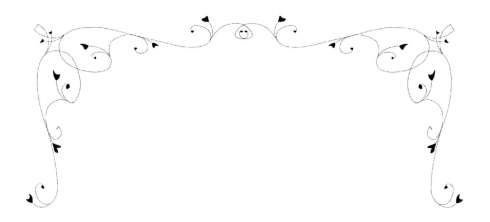

Soups and Salads

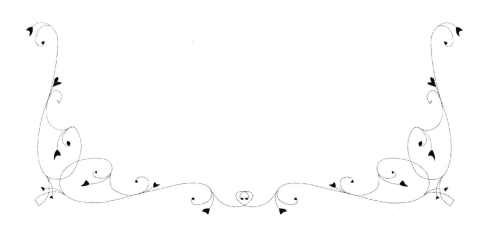

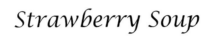

Strawberry Soup

This recipe came from Micki, she preps our sandwiches, does dishes and is a jack-of-all-trades.

- ½ c. orange juice
- 6 oz. vanilla yogurt
- 6 oz. strawberry yogurt
- 3 c. fresh strawberries
- 2 T. honey
- ¼ t. nutmeg
- ½ t. cinnamon
- Mint leaves and sliced strawberries for garnish

In food processor puree strawberries. Add vanilla and strawberry yogurt, orange juice, honey and spices. Puree until very smooth. Chill. Stand mint leaf up on one side of dish and float a thin slice of strawberry on top. Serve very cold. Enjoy on a hot summer day!

Makes about 3½ cups.

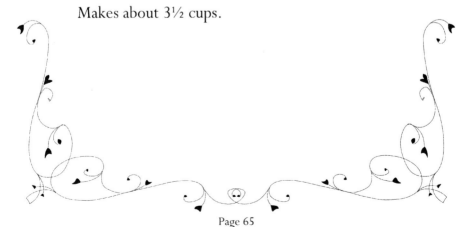

Notes

Peach Soup

This recipe is an adaptation of the Strawberry Soup. The peaches add a wonderfully unique flavor.

- ½ c. orange juice
- 6 oz. vanilla yogurt
- 6 oz. peach yogurt
- 3 c. fresh peaches (or canned)
- 2 T. honey
- ¼ t. nutmeg
- ½ t. cinnamon
- Mint leaves for garnish

In food processor puree peaches. Add vanilla and peach yogurt, orange juice, honey and spices. Puree until very smooth. Chill. Stand mint leaf up on one side of dish. Serve very cold. Enjoy on a hot summer day!

Makes about 3½ cups.

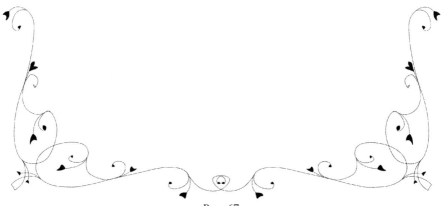

Notes

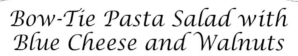

Bow-Tie Pasta Salad with Blue Cheese and Walnuts

This is one of my favorites! Carla, our head cook, described the ingredients in the recipe. She made me so hungry, I told her she had to make it and bring it in for me. I knew it would be great and it certainly is!

- 3 c. bow tie pasta
- 1 c. blue cheese
- ½ c. golden raisins
- 1 c. fresh basil chopped, must be fresh!
- Olive oil
- Salt and pepper

Cook pasta according to directions. Drain. Add cheese, raisins and basil. Toss lightly. Add just enough olive oil to hold pasta together and season to taste.

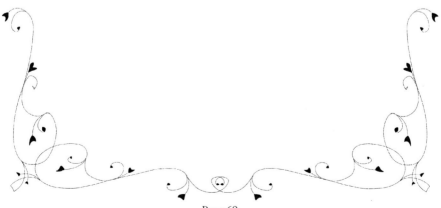

Notes

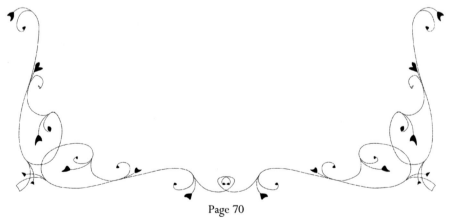

Carla's Potato, Cucumber and Dill Salad

- 3 lg. potatoes, unpeeled and sliced thinly
- ¼ c. rice vinegar
- ¼ c. canola oil
- 1 ½ T. dijon mustard
- ½ c. dill, chopped or 1 T. dried dill
- 1 lg. cucumber, unpeeled and sliced thinly
- Salt and pepper to taste

In 9" square dish, place potatoes in dish and cover with plastic wrap. Cook 9-11 minutes in microwave stirring gently every 3 minutes. In a small jar or plastic container with lid, combine vinegar, oil, mustard, dill. Shake well and pour over potatoes. Cover and chill until cool. Gently mix in cucumbers and serve.

Makes about 4 servings.

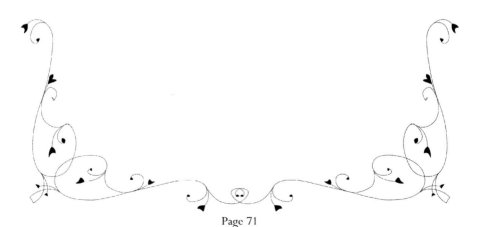

Notes

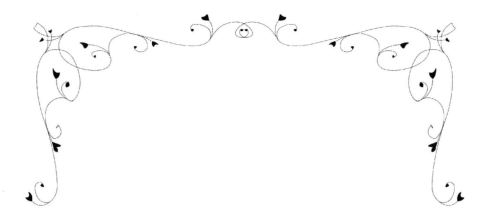

Desserts

Chocolate Snaps

- 1 pkg. of Devil's Food Cake Mix
- ⅓ c. oil
- 2 eggs, lightly beaten
- 1 t. ground ginger
- ½ t. pepper
- 1 t. cinnamon
- 1 T. water
- ¾ c. chocolate chips
- ¼ c. sugar

Preheat oven to 375°. Combine first 7 ingredients in a large bowl. Mix until smooth. Stir in chocolate chips. Shape dough into 1 inch balls; roll in sugar to coat. Place balls 2 inches apart on a lightly greased baking sheet. Bake for 9 minutes. Cool 2-3 minutes on baking sheets before removing to wire racks to cool completely. Makes about 4 dozen.

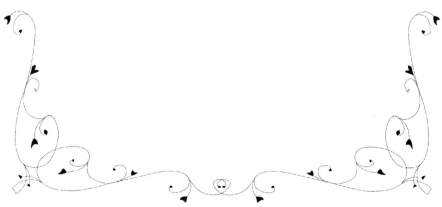

Notes

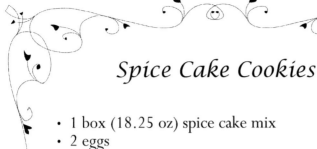

Spice Cake Cookies

- 1 box (18.25 oz) spice cake mix
- 2 eggs
- ½ c. unsalted butter, melted
- 2 T. flour
- 1 c. white chocolate chips
- ½ c. chopped pecans

Glaze

- 1 c. white chocolate chips melted

Preheat oven to 350°. Line baking sheets with parchment paper. In a large bowl, combine cake mix, eggs, melted butter and flour. Stir in chocolate chips and nuts. Drop dough by rounded tablespoons. Bake for 7-10 minutes or until done.

To make glaze:

Melt white chocolate chips in the microwave at ½ power for 20 seconds. Stir well beating with a spoon. Put back into microwave and do 20 seconds more. If still not melted, do again until all the chips are melted. Stir again. Drizzle cooled cookies with melted white chocolate.

Notes

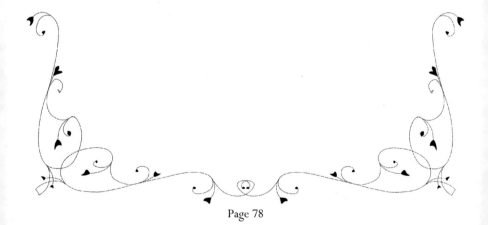

Lemon Poppy Seed Coookies

- 1 box lemon cake mix
- 2 T. poppy seeds
- 2½ T. flour
- 1 T. lemon juice
- 1 T. lime juice
- 2 eggs
- 2 c. white chocolate chips, (divided – 1 c. for cookies, 1 c. for glaze)
- ½ c. butter, melted

Mix cake mix, poppy seeds and flour. Add lemon and lime juice, eggs, and melted butter, just until blended. Stir in 1 c. white chocolate chips. Scoop out 1 inch balls onto lightly sprayed cookie sheet pan. Bake at 350° for about 7 minutes or until set in center. Glaze with melted white chocolate chips. (Hint: To melt white chocolate chips in the microwave, mix in 1-2 t. canola oil. Microwave at 50% power for 20 seconds. Stir and microwave again until melted. Be sure to use 50% power otherwise the chips burn and become hard.)

Notes

Peppermint Pats

- ¾ c. butter
- ¼ c. sugar
- 1 egg
- 1 t. vanilla
- 2 t. peppermint extract
- 2 c. flour
- ½ c. finely crushed hard peppermint candy
- Red decorator sugar crystals

Beat butter with a mixer until soft and creamy. Gradually add ¼ c. sugar, beating well. Add egg, beat well. Stir in extract and vanilla. Gradually add flour; mix well. Stir in candy. Shape dough into 2 logs about 12 inches each. Roll in sugar crystals; wrap logs in parchment paper and freeze until firm. Slice logs into ½ inch slices and place on ungreased baking sheets. Bake at 350° for 8-10 minutes or until done. Cool on pan for a few minutes and transfer to a cooling rack.

Makes about 4 dozen.

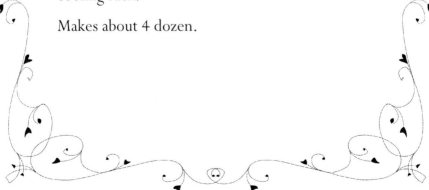

Notes

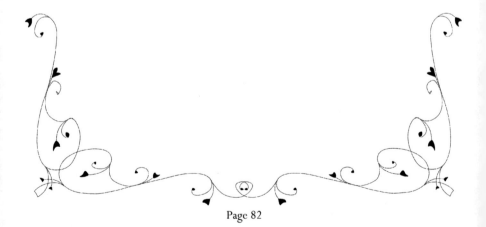

Lemon Blossom Cookies

- 1 c. butter
- ½ c. granulated sugar
- ½ c. brown sugar
- 1 egg
- 1 t. lemon peel, grated
- 1 T. lemon juice
- 1½ t. pure vanilla extract
- ¼ t. baking soda
- ¼ t. salt
- 2½ c. flour

Glaze:

- 1¼ c. powdered sugar
- 1 t. vanilla
- ½ t. lemon peel
- 2-4 t. lemon juice

Preheat oven to 400°. Cream butter, sugar, and brown sugar together. Add egg, lemon peel, lemon juice, and vanilla. Beat at medium speed in mixer until light and fluffy. Add flour, baking soda, and salt. Beat at low speed until soft dough forms. Bake for 5 minutes or until set. Cool completely and frost with lemon glaze.

Notes

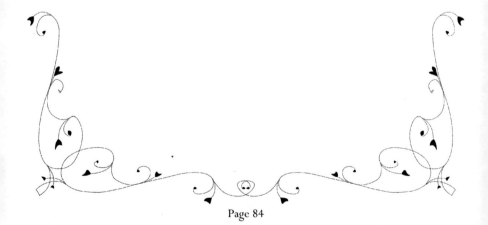

Lemon Blossom Cookies
Continued

For glaze:

Combine glaze ingredients and beat at low speed with electric mixer until smooth. Spread or drizzle on cookies. Let dry completely before storing.

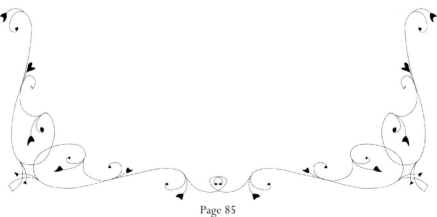

Notes

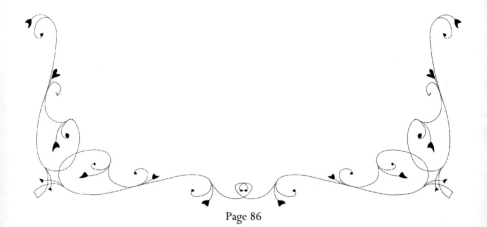

Perfectly Chocolatey Cookies

- 1 c. unsalted butter
- ¾ c. sugar
- 1 c. brown sugar
- 1 t. vanilla
- 2 eggs
- ⅓ c. unsweetened cocoa powder
- 1 t. baking soda
- ½ t. salt
- 2¼ c. flour
- 1 c. semi sweet chocolate chips
- 1 c. white chocolate chips
- 1 c. chopped walnuts (optional) or ½ c. chopped toffee candy bar

Preheat oven to 375°. Cream butter, sugars, and vanilla on medium speed of mixer. Add eggs and beat until smooth. Gradually add the dry ingredients. Stir in chocolate chips and nuts. Drop by rounded teaspoonfuls onto ungreased cookie sheet. Bake 8 minutes. Cool slightly and move to wire rack.

Notes

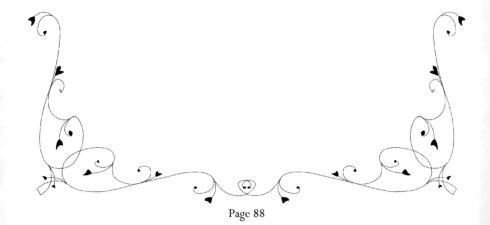

Fresh Mint Chocolate Chip Cookies

- 1⅓ c. sugar
- ¾ c. butter, softened
- 4 T. mint leaves, finely chopped
- 1 egg
- 2 c. flour
- 1 t. baking soda
- ½ t. salt
- 1 pkg. (12 oz.) semi-sweet chocolate chips

Preheat oven to 350°. Beat sugar, butter, mint leaves and egg in a large bowl. Stir in flour, baking soda and salt. Stir in chocolate chips.

Drop dough by rounded tablespoon about 2 inches apart onto an ungreased cookie sheet. Bake 11-13 minutes or until golden brown. Cool about 2 minutes; remove from cookie sheet.

Makes about 3½ dozen cookies.

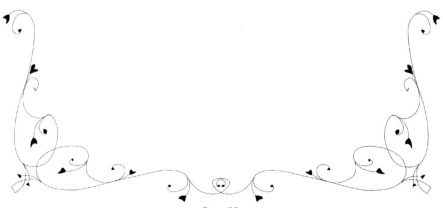

Notes

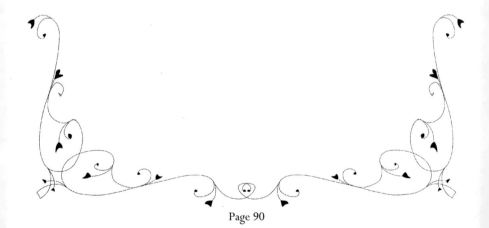

Cranberry Orange Bliss Cookies

- 1 c. cranberries, dried
- 1 c. white chocolate chips
- 2 c. butter, softened
- 1 c. sugar
- 1 c. brown sugar
- 2 eggs
- 2 t. orange peel, grated
- 2 T. orange juice (or cranberry juice)
- 3 t. pure vanilla extract
- ½ t. baking soda
- ½ t. salt
- 5 c. flour

Glaze:

- 1¼ c. powdered sugar
- 1-2 t. pure vanilla extract
- 1 t. orange peel, grated
- 2-4 t. orange juice

Preheat oven to 375°. Cream butter, sugar and brown sugar together. Add eggs, orange peel, orange juice and vanilla. Beat at medium speed in mixer until light and fluffy. Add flour, baking soda and salt. Beat at low speed until soft dough forms. Bake for 5-6 minutes. Cool completely

Notes

Cranberry Orange Bliss Cookies Continued

and frost with orange glaze.

For glaze:

Mix powdered sugar, vanilla, orange peel and orange juice to desired consistency. Beat at low speed with an electric mixer until smooth. Drizzle on cookies. Let dry completely before storing.

Notes

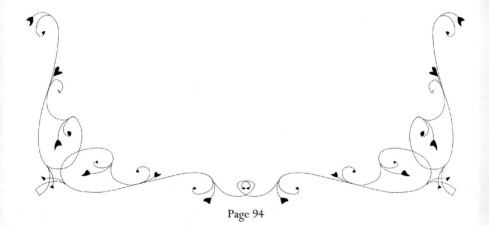

Lemon Cake

- 1 pkg. white cake mix
- 1 small pkg. instant lemon pudding
- 4 eggs
- ¼ c. fresh lemon juice
- ¼ c. lime juice
- Zest of 2 lemons
- Zest of 2 limes
- ½ c. buttermilk
- ⅓ c. oil

Glaze

- 1 lb. powdered sugar
- Lemon juice, fresh (or lime juice)
- Lemon zest

Mix together all ingredients. Beat until all lumps are gone, about 3 minutes with a hand mixer. Spray mini bundt pans with floured spray. Scoop out cake batter and place into mini bundt pans. Bake at 350° for 7-9 minutes or until a toothpick comes out clean when inserted. Glaze when completely cool.

Glaze:

Notes

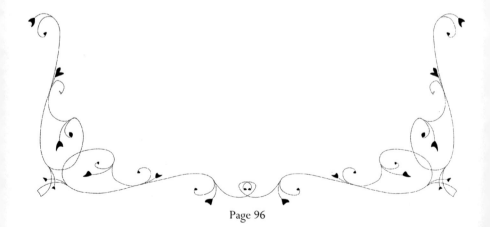

Lemon Cake Continued

Place a 1 lb. pkg of powdered sugar into a
mixing bowl. Gradually beat in enough fresh
lemon juice and/or lime juice to make desired
consistency for dipping. Add the zest of 1
lemon. Dip cooled cakes into glaze. Let dry
completely before covering.

Notes

Chocolate Mocha Chip Mini Cakes

- 1 chocolate cake mix
- 1 lg. pkg. instant chocolate pudding
- 1 c. buttermilk
- 4 eggs
- ½ c. oil
- ½ c. strong coffee
- 2 c. semi sweet chocolate chips

Glaze

- 1 lb. powered sugar
- ⅓ c. Dutch processed cocoa
- Hot water

Preheat oven to 350°. Mix together first six ingredients. Beat until well mixed about 3 minutes. Fold in chocolate chips. Spray mini bundt pans with flour spray. Fill pans with batter about two-thirds full. Bake about 10-13 minutes or until done with a toothpick. Cool completely before glazing. Makes about 36 mini bundt cakes. These freeze very well.

For glaze:

Mix sugar and cocoa together. Gradually add 2-4 T. hot water until desired consistency. Drizzle over cakes or make the glaze thin enough so you can actually dip the cooled cakes into the glaze.

Notes

Maple Spice Cakes

- 1 stick unsalted butter, at room temperature
- 1 ⅓ cups packed light brown sugar
- 2 eggs, room temperature
- ⅓ c. pure maple syrup
- 2 ½ c. cake flour
- 1 ½ t. cinnamon
- 1 t. baking powder
- 1 t. baking soda
- 1 t. ground allspice
- ¾ t. ground ginger
- ½ t. salt
- 1 c. buttermilk

Glaze

- 4 c. powdered sugar
- ½ c. maple syrup
- 1-2 t. maple extract
- Water to desired consistency

Preheat oven to 350°. Spray mini bundt pans or maple leaf pans with flour spray.

In a large bowl using an electric mixer, cream the butter with the brown sugar until fluffy. Add the eggs one at a time, beating well after each

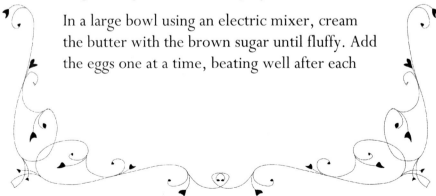

Notes

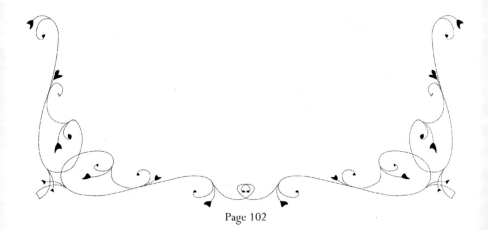

Maple Spice Cakes
Continued

addition. Beat in the maple syrup. In a medium bowl, whisk the cake flour with the cinnamon, baking powder, baking soda, allspice, ginger and salt. Mix the dry ingredients into the batter in three additions, alternating with the buttermilk. Fill pans about two-thirds full with batter. Bake 10-13 minutes or until done with toothpick. Cool completely on wire racks before glazing.

For glaze:

Mix sugar, maple syrup and extract together. Add water until desired consistency. Drizzle over cakes or make the glaze thin enough so you can actually dip the cooled cakes into the glaze.

Makes about 36 mini cakes.

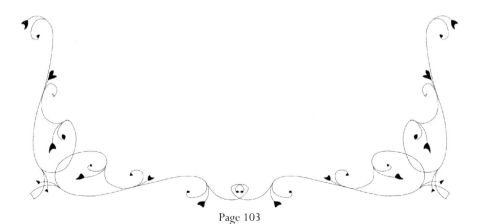

Notes

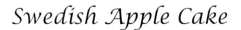

Swedish Apple Cake

- 1 (21 oz.) can apple pie filling (or make your own like we do – recipe to follow)
- 1 spice cake mix
- 3 lg. eggs
- ⅓ c. oil
- 1¼ c. water

Sauce

- 1 c. brown sugar
- 2 T. flour
- Pinch of nutmeg
- ¼ t. cinnamon
- ⅛ t. salt
- 1 c. water
- 2 T. butter

Grease a 9"x13" pan. Preheat oven to 350°. Spread 1 can of apple pie filling or about 4 c. homemade filling into pan. In large bowl, mix together cake mix, eggs, oil and water. Beat 2 minutes. Pour on top of apple filling. Bake until cake springs back in center about 25-35 minutes. Cut and place into dishes. Serve warm with warm sauce poured over the top. Enjoy!

Notes

Swedish Apple Cake
Continued

Sauce:

Place sauce ingredients in a small saucepan. Stir together and cook until mixture becomes thickened. Serve over cake.

Notes

Homemade Apple Pie Filling

- 4-6 apples, chopped, leave peel on if desired
- ⅓ c. sugar
- ⅓ c. brown sugar
- 3 T. flour
- ½ t. cinnamon
- ¼ t. cloves
- 2 t. lemon juice
- 1 c. water

Mix all ingredients together in a sauce pan. Cook over medium heat for about 15 minutes stirring occasionally. Reduce heat and simmer until apples are tender and sauce has thickened. Cool.

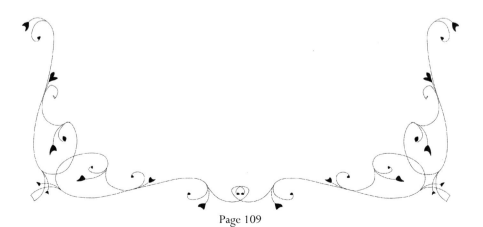

Notes

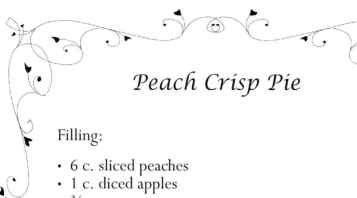

Peach Crisp Pie

Filling:

- 6 c. sliced peaches
- 1 c. diced apples
- ¾ c. sugar
- ¼ c. flour
- 1 t. nutmeg
- 1 t. cinnamon
- 1 t. grated lemon peel

Crumb topping:

- ½ c. butter softened
- ¾ c. brown sugar
- 1 c. flour
- 1 t. cinnamon
- ½ t. nutmeg
- ½ c. quick cooking oats

Double pie crust:

- 1½ sticks Crisco butter flavored shortening sticks
- 2 t. salt
- 3 c. flour

Preheat oven to 350°. Cut butter with a pastry cutter until crumbly mixture forms. Add the ½

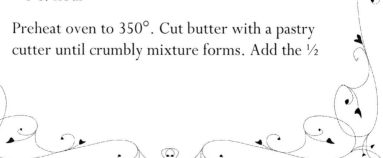

Notes

Peach Crisp Pie Continued

c. warm water and mix with hands until it forms a soft ball of dough. Add a little flour and knead until it is smooth enough to roll out.

Spray the bottom of a large pan with cooking spray. Add the peach filling to the bottom of the pan. Top with the crumb topping and cover with the pie crust. Add slits on top of the pie crust for steam to escape while baking the pie. Bake for about 30 minutes.

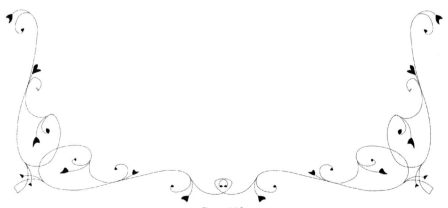

Notes

Blackberry Pie

- 1¼ c. sugar
- ¼ c. flour
- ¼ t. salt
- 4 c. blackberries, fresh or frozen

Crust

- 1½ sticks butter Crisco
- 2 t. salt
- 3 c. flour
- ½ c. water, warm

Preheat oven to 375°. Combine sugar, flour and salt. Add sugar mixture to blackberries and mix well. Fill pie crust with mixture. Cover with top layer of crust. Bake for 35 minutes or until crust is golden brown. Cool on a wire rack.

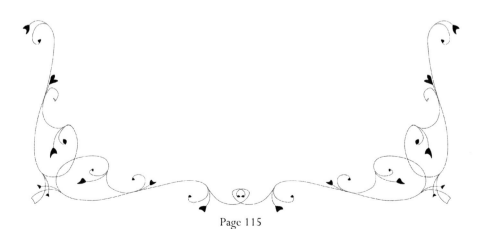

Notes

Pear Crumble Pie

Filling

- ½ c. sugar
- 2 T. flour
- 1 t. lemon peel, finely grated
- 5 c. pears, sliced (fresh or canned)

Crumb Mixture

- ½ c. flour
- ½ c. sugar
- 1 t. ginger, ground
- 1 t. cinnamon, ground
- ¼ c. butter

Crust

- 1½ sticks butter Crisco
- 2 t. salt
- 3 c. flour
- ½ c. water, warm

Preheat oven to 375°. Combine sugar, flour and lemon peel. In a large bowl sprinkle pears; toss to coat them. Pour the filling over the pie crust. In a separate bowl combine the flour, sugar and spices. Cut in butter until it resembles coarse crumbs. Sprinkle the crumb mixture over the pear filling. Bake for 35 minutes or until crust is golden brown. Cool on a wire rack.

Notes

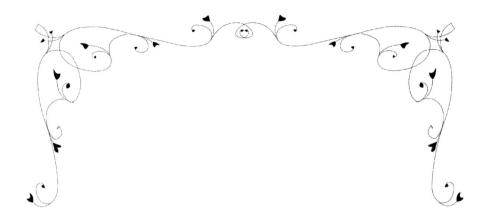

Scones and Condiments

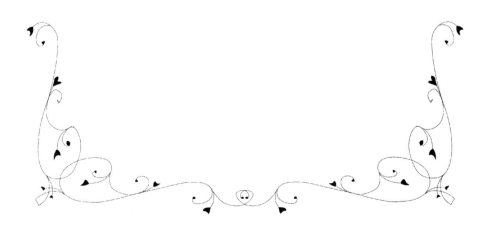

Tips on Making Scones

Use quality ingredients.

Use cold butter; don't let it soften. Cold butter makes the scones rise higher.

Drain fruit very well.

Add fruit last, barely mix it in to flour mixture.

Add only enough buttermilk to make dough stick together.

If dough is too sticky when you pat it on the floured board, add more flour.

If dough is too dry and crumbles when you try and pat it on the floured board, add more buttermilk.

If you are using frozen fruit, make sure it does not thaw out. Mix it in quickly and cut scones fast. If it thaws out, the dough is very sticky and a mess!

Make sure oven is hot and preheated to 400°.

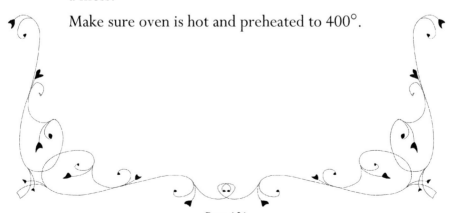

Cranberry Orange Scones

- 3 c. self-rising flour
- ½ c. sugar
- 1 stick unsalted butter
- ¾ c. - 1 c. buttermilk
- ¼ c. orange juice
- ½ c. chopped cranberries (use fresh, freeze until firm and then chop in food processor)
- Zest of 1 orange

Glaze:

- 1 c. powdered sugar
- 2-3 T. orange juice

Preheat oven to 400°. Combine flour and sugar. Cut in butter until mixture is coarse and crumbly. Add cranberries and orange zest or peel. Add orange juice to ½ c. buttermilk. Stir this mixture into the flour mixture to make a soft dough. If mixture is too dry, add more buttermilk. Turn out on a floured board, form into a circle and cut into 8 pie shaped wedges.

Place scones on a cookie sheet. Bake until lightly browned about 10 minutes. Brush with glaze while still hot.

Notes

Cranberry Orange Scones
Continued

May be reheated in foil.

Makes 10-15 scones.

Notes

Jamaican Lime Scones

- 3 c. self-rising flour
- ½ c. sugar
- 1 stick unsalted butter
- ½ c. buttermilk
- ¼ c. lime juice
- Zest of 1 lime

Glaze:

- ⅛ c. sweetened coconut
- ½ c. packed brown sugar
- 4 t. butter, melted
- 4 t. lime juice
- 4 t. rum or ⅛ t. rum extract
- ½ c. toasted chopped pecans

Preheat oven to 400°. Combine flour and sugar.
Cut in butter until mixture is coarse and
crumbly. Add limeade and lime juice, and zest.
Gradually stir in enough buttermilk (about ½ c.)
to make a soft dough. If mixture is too dry, add
more buttermilk. Turn out on a floured board,
form into a circle and cut into 8 pie shaped
wedges.

Place scones on a cookie sheet. Bake until lightly

Notes

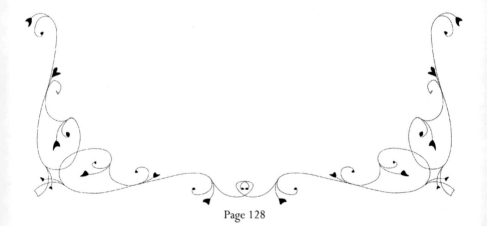

Jamaican Lime Scones
Continued

browned about 10 minutes. May be reheated in foil.

For glaze: Combine all glaze ingredients except for pecans. Dip cooled scone into glaze or drizzle on top. Sprinkle with toasted pecans.

Makes 10 to 15 scones.

Notes

Anniversary Scones with a Twist

This is a variation of our raspberry anniversary scones. Blackberries add a different flavor. If the blackberries are too big, cut them in half. Just be careful when you add the buttermilk. Add only enough buttermilke to make a soft dough. Don't stir, but fold gently, otherwise your scones will be purple.

- 3 c. self-rising flour
- ½ c. sugar
- 1 stick unsalted butter
- ¾ -1 c. buttermilk
- ½ c. blackberries
- ½ c. white chocolate
- ¼ c. coconut

Preheat oven to 400°. Combine flour and sugar. Cut in butter until mixture is coarse and crumbly. Add white chocolate, coconut and blackberries. Fold in ½ c. buttermilk very gently into the flour mixture to make a soft dough. If mixture is too dry, add more buttermilk. Turn dough out on a floured board, form into a circle and cut into 8 pie shaped wedges.

Notes

Anniversary Scones with a Twist Continued

Place scones on a cookie sheet. Bake until lightly browned about 10 minutes. Brush with glaze while still hot.

May be reheated in foil.

Makes 10-15 scones.

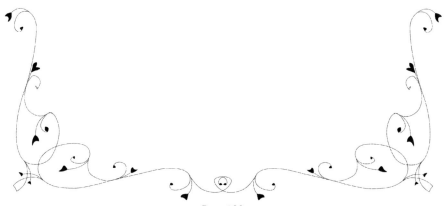

Notes

Lemon Curd

- ½ c. butter
- 1 c. granulated sugar
- ½ c. lemon juice
- 1½ t. grated lemon zest
- 3 eggs

Melt butter in microwave for 1 minute. Beat eggs in a glass bowl with an electric mixer until frothy. Mix in butter, sugar, lemon juice and zest. Microwave on HIGH for 3 minutes.

Beat mixture again until smooth. Microwave on HIGH for another 3 minutes. Beat mixture again until smooth. Refrigerate until set/cool. Lemon curd will keep up to 2 weeks in refrigerator.

Makes about 1 cup of lemon curd.

Notes

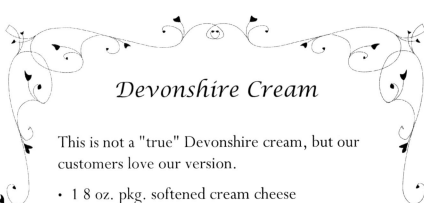

Devonshire Cream

This is not a "true" Devonshire cream, but our customers love our version.

- 1 8 oz. pkg. softened cream cheese
- 2 c. powdered sugar
- ½ freshly squeezed lemon
- 2 t. vanilla
- 1 c. sour cream

In a small bowl with an electric mixer, beat cream cheese, lemon juice, and vanilla. Gradually beat in powdered sugar. Fold in sour cream.

Makes 1½ cups.

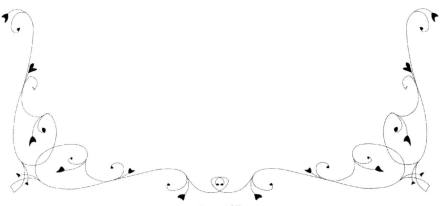

Notes

Index

Index Continued

Index Continued

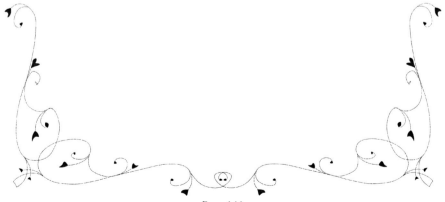

About the Author

Amy Lawrence began her tea room in August of 2003. Previously she had been a special education teacher for 11 years teaching learning disabled and autistic students. She took a two year break to be home with her two sons. In August of 2002 while having tea with my mother, she said, "This is what I want to do now! I want my own tea room. I love to cook and have always enjoyed catering for special parties." In November of 2002, she attended a tea conference and also became a certified tea consultant. It all began from there. With the help of dedicated family and friends, she finally opened her tea room on August 27, 2003. In July 2006, Tea Experience Digest named An Afternoon to Remember Tea Parlor and Gifts the Reader's Choice Award for Best Small City Tea Room in the U.S. At the present time, Amy has self-published 4 cookbooks and is currently working on a new book on afternoon teas.

Printed in the United States
213047BV00002B/2/A

9 780979 617034